ILKESTON & GLOSSOP TRAMWAYS

Barry M Marsden

Series editor Robert J Harley

MP Middleton Press

Cover pictures -
Front cover: Please see caption 47.   Back cover: please see caption 65.

Published July 2004

ISBN 1 904474 40 3

© *Middleton Press, 2004*

Design   Deborah Esher
           David Pede
Published by
           Middleton Press
           Easebourne Lane
           Midhurst, West Sussex
           GU29 9AZ
Tel: 01730 813169
Fax: 01730 812601
Email: info@middletonpress.co.uk
www.middletonpress.co.uk

Printed & bound by Biddles Ltd, Kings Lynn

Ilkeston Tramways 1-60   *Glossop Tramways 61-120*

PART 1 – ILKESTON TRAMWAYS

Opening of the Electric Tramway	1	White Lion Square	42
Cotmanhay Terminus	5	Park Road Tram Depot	44
Cotmanhay Road	12	Nottingham Road.	49
Granby Street	16	Thurman Street.	52
Bath Street	17	Corporation Road.	53
Station Road Spur	28	Hallam Fields Terminus	54
Market Place	31	Refurbishment.	58
South Street	39		

INTRODUCTION AND ACKNOWLEDGEMENTS

The Ilkeston Corporation Tramway was the first electric tramway system in Derbyshire, opening on 16th May 1903, over a year before its much larger neighbour, Derby, and as such a real focus of civic pride. The Glossop undertaking commenced the following August, and was the second of its kind in the county. Both enterprises were remarkably similar in origin, though the first was a corporation facility, the second a private one. Both operated on mainly single line and loop track, with a route length of between 3.5 and 4.5 miles (5.6 and 7.2 km) and initially deploying between seven and nine open-top cars. Both clung to the very edges of the county, the former in the south-east, the latter in the north-west, and both lay within or near to extensive valleys, the Erewash and the Longdendale. Both systems served fairly small and static populations, and there was even some similarity in the layouts, as each included a main track with a single spur, and each employed double deck open toppers with reversed staircases, though running on different gauges.

For the photographs of the Ilkeston tramway I am indebted to the late David and Eddie Harrison, the Erewash Museum, Ilkeston Public Library, Andrew Knighton and G.H.F. Atkins. Glynn Waite kindly supplied pictures of the Ilkeston tickets from his own collection.

GEOGRAPHICAL SETTING

Situated in the south-east corner of Derbyshire, Ilkeston occupies a hilltop position overlooking the Erewash Valley to the east, the river forming the boundary between Derbyshire and Nottinghamshire. The Nutbrook Canal to the west and the Erewash Canal to the east attest to the former importance of water-borne transport, but in the early 20th century coal mining was the major source of employment, though the metal founding industry was well represented, and textile and clothing factories provided a good deal of work for the local population. The area was well served by the rail network, and both the Midland and Great Northern Railways had stations situated in and around the town.

HISTORICAL BACKGROUND

By the early 1890s the corporation of Ilkeston saw the need for an effective system of transport to serve the borough of some 30,000 souls. Plans were drawn up for an electric tramline, which would run from Cotmanhay in the north of the township to Hallam Fields in the south-east, a distance of some 3.5 miles. A spur line would run east off the main track some half-mile to the Ilkeston Junction railway station over the Erewash, and the gauge was set at 3ft 6ins (1067mm). Work began on the tracklaying in December 1901, and land was purchased for a tram shed and offices on Park Road. The line was the usual single track and turnout system, with a steep 1 in 12 (8.3%) gradient up Bath Street, and laid down the centre of the main thoroughfares.

The track was almost certainly laid by November 1902, and the overhead *in situ* when the first of the original nine tramcars were delivered in a livery of chocolate and cream. They were built by the Electric Railway and Tramway Carriage Company of Preston, a subsidiary of Dick, Kerr, and were open-top double-deckers of the 'Preston' model, with reversed stairs and running on rigid four wheel, Brill 21E trucks of a 6ft (1828mm) wheelbase. By early 1903 all was in readiness for operations, but despite promises, the power, to be supplied by a locally built station, the Derbyshire and Nottinghamshire Power Company, was unavailable. The company lagged months behind schedule, and did not connect up the vital electric cables until 1st May.

The opening ceremony took place on 16th May, with an official trip by Cars 5 and 6 along the system, and so many passengers rode the line during the first weeks that the manager, Oscar Pilcher, was fooled into thinking that these levels would be maintained indefinitely. Consequently he persuaded the tramway committee to invest in four further trams, which were really not needed. These were supplied by British Westinghouse, with Milnes Voss bodies, and were outwardly indistinguishable from the earlier models, apart from their electrics. After the early euphoria the undertaking settled down to an unremarkable existence, with passenger numbers remaining steady, and deficits slowly and inexorably rising. Deficiencies in the original construction led to costly repairs to the track and frequent renewal of the running wire, whilst several pleas to the Board of Trade to top-cover the conveyances went unheeded. The trams too had to be thoroughly overhauled in 1910, and their leaky roofs replaced.

World War I had a deleterious effect on the system, with shortages of equipment leading to deterioration in the fleet vehicles, track and overhead, whilst staff shortages due to the conflict led to the recruitment of women to replace male conductors. However, in 1916 the council pulled off a brilliant coup, by selling the facility to the recently established Nottinghamshire and Derbyshire Tramways Company (NDTC), who operated a 15 mile (24.1 km) route between Ripley and Nottingham. The bait was the prospect of joining the former to the latter at Heanor after the war.

In 1919 Balfour, Beatty, who owned the NDTC rationalised the Ilkeston car fleet after all the 13 trams had been refurbished at their Langley Mill depot. After a thorough overhaul five trams were sent to other Balfour, Beatty systems, whilst the remaining eight were given direct stairs and the company livery of light green and cream. The NDTC proposed uniting the two tramlines in 1922, but despite securing Parliamentary assent, the costly proposal was never effected. The NDTC began developing a motorbus enterprise, and saw that the trolleybus would be a viable replacement for the ageing tramcar on both facilities.

The Ilkeston tramway limped on until the early 30s, before it was finally closed down. In 1924, Car 7 was cut down to single-deck configuration to serve on the Junction spur after revamping at Langley Mill, and in 1928, the parent company secured powers to replace the trams with trackless vehicles. In December 1930 they commenced removing the Ilkeston tracks, though the enterprise did not finally expire until 8th January 1931, when Car 5 took the town's *prominenti* on a final shortened run, ending up at the tram shed in a blinding snowstorm!

The following day motorbuses took over the route, whilst the rails were lifted and the overhead converted for trolleybus operation. A year later the first single-deck AEC and EE railless commenced services from Cotmanhay to Hallam Fields, and the following August the first trolleybus pioneered the run from Ilkeston to Heanor, linking up the two undertakings, and fulfilling the original dreams of the NDTC envisaged as far back as 1903. Yet the trolleybuses only lasted for 20 years, until they were finally supplanted by the all powerful motorbus.

OPENING OF THE ELECTRIC TRAMWAY.

1. The original plan of the Ilkeston Tramway showed a short section of track crossing the Erewash Canal at bottom right, which was never actually constructed. It was intended as the entrance to a car shed which was eventually built on Park Road.

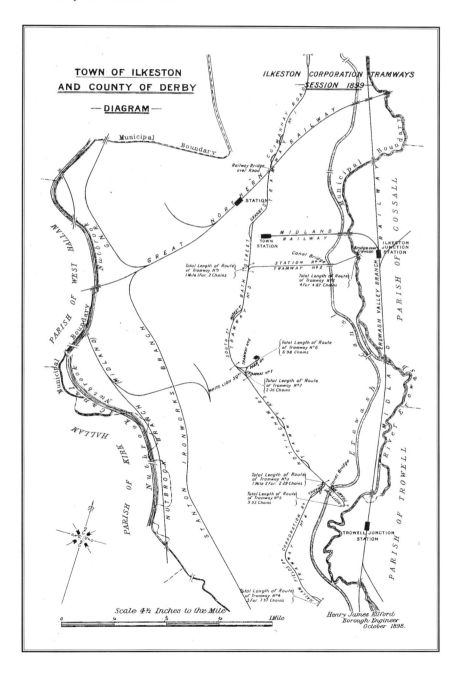

2. Cars 5 and 6, suitably bedecked with flags and bunting and loaded with councillors and other *prominenti,* wait on the Town Hall loop for orders to proceed. Note the Mayoral party on a first floor balcony with the Mayor, Alderman Sudbury, addressing the gathering. The date is 16th May 1903.

3. Surrounded by a huge throng of celebrating Il'sonians, including one in a top hat, Car 5 prepares to move off the Market Place turnout. On the platform of the packed vehicle is Alderman Sudbury, very much a King Edward VII lookalike!

4. Car 5 moves gingerly off the loop on its way north to Cotmanhay, gliding smoothly past the large celebratory crowds who massed at various points along the route.

COTMANHAY TERMINUS

5. Cotmanhay was the northern terminus of the system, and this opening day scene reveals Cars 5 and 6 parked side-by-side on the twin track. The Methodist Chapel stands on the right, and a solitary policeman oversees the diversely apparelled crowd.

6. Car 4 at Cotmanhay, displaying a dented dash panel, and a good window display that includes an advert for 'Rose Day', presumably at one of the three annual Ilkeston flower shows. Note the vision slot cut in the staircase riser to give the motorman a view to his otherwise blind left side.

7. Milnes Car 13 was a popular subject for local cameramen, and in this view it pauses at Cotmanhay for its photograph. Again the vision slot is well seen. Two differences between the Preston and Milnes trams were in the variant angles of the handbrake handles, and design differences in the tops of the sheet metal staircase panels above the drivers' heads.

8. Car 13 again at Cotmanhay, giving a good view of the Brill truck, and another dented dash. The name of the manager, L.F. Bellamy, puts the date in the 1913-16 era, and the time of year, judging by the chapel harvest festival notice, is early autumn. Note that the conductor still has to reverse most of the top-deck seat backs for the return trip to town.

9. Car 13 still sports its damaged dash panel at Cotmanhay in this wartime shot, with the top-deck soldier and the union flag on the platform bulkhead by the conductor's left arm, on a collection box for the Relief Fund sponsored by the Tramways Committee in early 1915. The motorman is J. D. Turton.

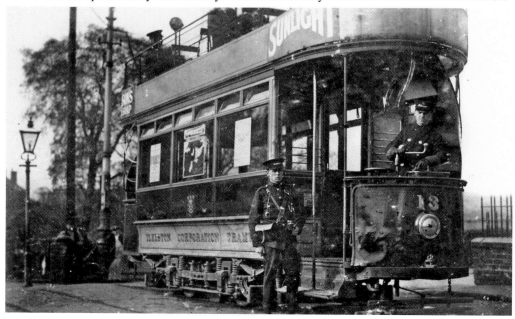

10. A worse-for-wear Car 8, with sagging platforms and other signs of hard use, waits at Cotmanhay with its mixed crew in 1917. The headlamp sports a wartime hooded cover, whilst the tree visible in the last shot has subsequently been cut down.

11. This amusing study, posed at Cotmanhay post-war, features a Preston tramcar with the altered staircases dating from 1919-20. The motorman on the right is George Miles, the conductor Tom McKeigue.

COTMANHAY ROAD

12.   Looking south towards town along Cotmanhay Road reveals the bracket poles carrying the overhead, and the single track in its bed of stone setts. The entrance to Portland Road can be seen on the left, whilst the procession, consisting mainly of women and girls in their best dresses and sporting union flags, suggests a patriotic event.

13. In 1906 it was decided to add a turnout on Cotmanhay Road at the end of Archer Street, and this busy scene, looking north, shows the loop in the course of construction. The stone setts are being laid in the foreground, whilst a tram pauses in the distance on its way to the terminus.

Two of the first tickets ever issued on the system, on the inaugural run on 16th May 1903. A 0000 was presented to the Mayor, Alderman Francis Sudbury.

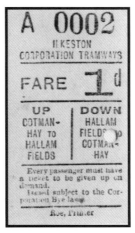

14. A lightly loaded Car 8 in its post World War I guise and livery, approaches the GNR Railway bridge over Cotmanhay Road on its way to town in 1928, passing the Charlotte Street loop on the right.

15. Looking north along Cotmanhay Road towards the GNR bridge from the junction with Granby Street on the left, and Awsworth Road on the right on a rainy day circa 1920. Side poles still carry the running wire, and the single line follows the road centre. The cast-iron urinal on the right, thoughtfully crowned by a streetlamp, has a distinctly continental flavour, and is being patronised by the local carter.

GRANBY STREET

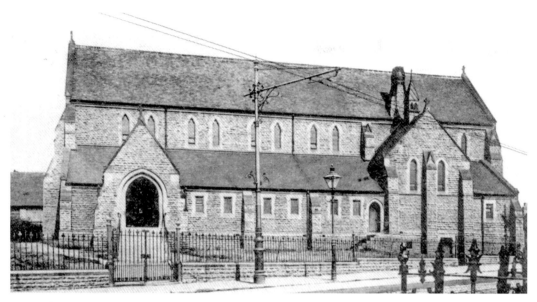

16. There is a dearth of photographs featuring this short stretch of thoroughfare, but this Valentine postcard depicts Holy Trinity Church, on the corner of Granby Street and Cotmanhay Road. The stone setts of the tramline appear at the bottom right, and a bracket pole carrying the twin overhead lines stands in front of the building.

One of the light blue penny tokens ordered for Corporation officials and others for travel on the tramway in 1911.

BATH STREET

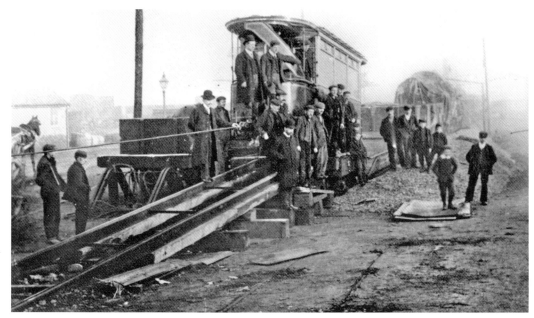

17. At the northern end of Bath Street was Heanor Road where the 'struck down' Preston tramcars arrived at the GNR goods depot. They were unloaded over the buffer stops and run along temporary rails to the foot of Bath Street, where they were towed to the depot along the tram track by steamroller. The tall bowler-hatted figure in front of one of the newly arrived cars is Tramway Manager, Oscar Pilcher, accompanied by his deputy, Arthur Gilbert.

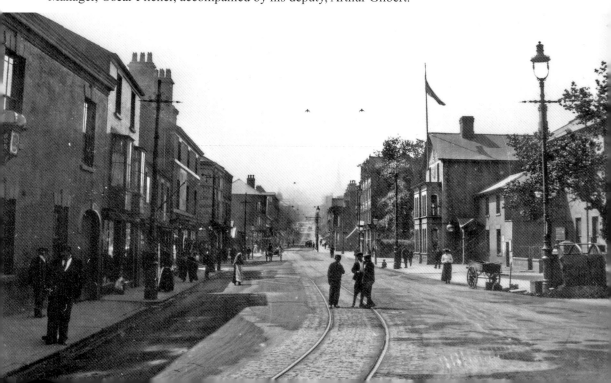

18. Looking up the 1 in 12 slope of Bath Street with the Rutland Hotel on the right. The Rutland loop is partly obscured by the group of lads posing on the track. Note the almost total lack of traffic on this usually busy main artery.

19. This opening day scene shows an overloaded Car 7 pausing on the Rutland loop, as a mass of would be riders attempt to embark, controlled by a single representative of the law. Here the overhead is carried on twin poles and span wire.

20. Car 4 is at rest in front of the Rutland Hotel in the early days of the service, a fact attested by the original clumsy 'cow-catcher' Stillgate lifeguards, which the Board of Trade ordered to be replaced by the more normal Tidswell pattern. Note the pristine state of the bodywork and truck, and the concertina metal gate blocking off the driver's platform.

21. A little further up Bath Street, at the junction with Pelham Street, one of the spanking new Preston trams is caught on a pre-service trial at the beginning of May 1903, showing off its lines outside Dexter's Furnishers.

22. The steepness of Bath Street can be appreciated in this view looking up the hill with a service car in the middle distance. Note the three ornate gas lamps outside the Trimming Shop on the left. In the distance can be seen the tall spire of the new Wesleyan Church, and beyond it the tower of St Mary's in the Market Place.

23. Some two weeks after the opening of the tramway, on 3rd June, General Sir John French, later C-in-C of British forces in France, unveiled a memorial plaque outside the Town Hall in honour of Ilkeston men who died in the Boer War. His carriage is shown ascending Bath Street, escorted by Car 2 and the local Yeomanry. Large crowds were present to give him an enthusiastic welcome. The white band on the right-hand traction pole indicated a tram stop.

←

24. Another fine and animated study of Bath Street early in the tram era reveals the Junction branch line curving right into Station Road, with Car 6 on the incline and a further vehicle on the far loop. Here the overhead runs directly across the road, and the extreme length of the bracket arm, which also supports the Junction wire, is worthy of note.

25. Car 1 grinds up Bath Street in this 1910 vista, taken just above Chapel Street on the right. William Fletcher, a vendor of wines and spirits whose premises appears on the left, also sold mineral waters and ginger beer, and was a well-known chemist. The metal shield on the nearest traction pole advertised the Mrs Bull magazine, 'a live paper for women.'

26. Decorated Car 5 heads down the Bath Street incline on the way to Cotmanhay on opening day, with Wilmot Street on the left, a shot taken from the upper deck of Car 6 following behind. Note that on this stretch the running wire was carried on ornate bracket arms down the right hand side of the road.

27. Car 12 takes the curve at the top of Bath Street by the Harrow Inn on the left, trolleyboom hard over to engage the overhead. A Girl Guide patrol marches on the left, and a large dog ambles nonchalantly in the right foreground.

STATION ROAD

28. A good study depicts Car 12 waiting at the upper end of Station Road, picking up trade for Ilkeston Junction, with Bath Street behind. Junction bound trams travelled from left to right down Bath Street from the depot, reversing trolleybooms to turn uphill onto the branch spur.

29. At the lower end of Station Road the same tram pauses at the Erewash Bridge terminus, ready for the uphill run to town. A summer date for the photograph is suggested by the motorman's white topped cap. Note how few advertisements are carried on this particular conveyance.

30. The author's impression gives an idea of the probable appearance of Car 7. It is shown, minus its upper deck and stairs, after its conversion around 1924 to a single decker on the Junction run.

MARKET PLACE

31. The single line climbs out of Bath Street and curves into the Market Place, with the points of the Town Hall loop visible in the foreground. The premises of the local Liberal Club can be seen behind the bracket posts, with the ivy-clad home of the local physician, Dr Wood, next door.

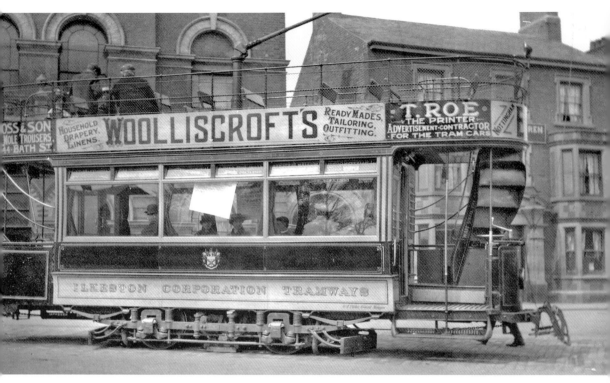

32. Car 1 in profile in front of the Town Hall, another early study, shows well the lengthy overhang of the tram body beyond the short wheelbase Brill truck, which led to a pitching ride. The Stillgate lifeguards are still in place, and a timetable adorns the centre window of the vehicle.

T. CLARK,
The People's DRAPER
150-152, Bath Street,
ILKESTON.
FIRST-CLASS DRESSMAKING.

Go to **CLARK'S**
for most up-to-date
Spring & Summer Goods
Now showing.

33. A later shot of Car 5 at the same venue reveals the replacement Tidswell lifeguards, and the closed folding platform gate. Note the window board showing COTMANHAY as the destination, and the police constable posed in front of the conveyance. The rope for swinging the trolleyboom can be clearly seen in this photograph.

34. Photographed from the Town Hall balcony circa 1908, this scene of a quiet Market Place picks out both the upperworks of a passing tramcar, and the layout of the loop.

35. Car 8, in a 1928 vintage picture, waits at the Market Place stop. Note the details of the Notts and Derby colours and the direct staircases. The window bills refer to an 'Open Meeting' and a chrysanthemum show.

36. A splendid shot taken at Ilkeston fair, with a superb view of the upper deck of one of the Preston cars and its swing back garden seats, posed in front of a magnificent merry-go-round. The photograph can be closely dated to the 21st-26th October 1909, when St Mary's Church in the background was having its tower dismantled to extend the nave.

37. Civic dignitaries pose at the Town Hall in front of Car 5, which carried them on a terminal run over part of the route on the evening of 8th January 1931. They include the Mayor, Councillor Beardsley, and his wife; Motorman Straw on the platform with Inspector O'Connor, Conductor Hodson, third on left, and Traffic Manager Laing, the tall central figure. The posters announce the withdrawal of the tram service.

38. The only remaining piece of tramway street furniture still *in situ* is this junction box, embellished with the Corporation coat of arms, and situated at the corner of the Market Place near St Mary's Church wall.

SOUTH STREET

39. South Street as it appeared circa 1909, with Car 7 heading north, and the Nag's Head pub on the immediate left next door to Hawkins' motor shop. The South Street schoolrooms can be seen lower down the road on the left.

40. Another exemplary study, taken further south along the same thoroughfare in the early part of the century, depicts Merry's Chemist's shop on the left. Figures pose in statuesque array for the cameramen, and the stone setts paving the permanent way stand out sharply.

41. Car 8, almost bereft of advertising, turns left into South Street from White Lion Square, the hub of the system. The window bill refers to a football match at the Manor ground, with a destination board visible below. Note the thatched cottage on the left, once the Rising Sun Inn, at the top of Derby Road, and sadly demolished in 1933.

WHITE LION SQUARE

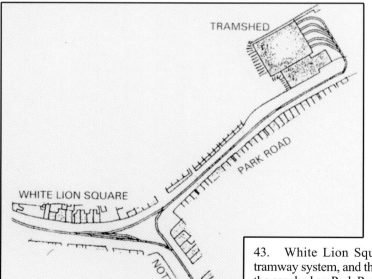

42. In the last picture Car 8 stands near where the white coated figure lurks, at the entrance to South Street. This scene was taken in 1905 from White Lion Square, and shows the tramline well to the roadside, with the running wire supported on twin poles. Dampier's Barbers, identified by its striped pole, is on the left at the entrance to Stanton Road, and the ex-Rising Sun thatched cottage appears to the right of the cart.

43. White Lion Square was the centre of the tramway system, and this plan shows it in relation to the car shed on Park Road. Using the triangular track arrangement in the square, cars could either turn right into South Street to Cotmanhay, or travel left down Nottingham Road to Hallam Fields.

PARK ROAD TRAM DEPOT

44. The classic façade is of the Tram Depot on Park Road, completed in 1903, with the car shed just visible on the far right. The building was described as having 'one of the most handsome frontages in the borough' and cost £6,950 to erect. Tramcars travelled left down Park Road to reach White Lion Square. The whole site has since been demolished.

45. A first rate picture shows Car 5 moving along the depot frontage on its way into town, with the Stillgate lifeguard proclaiming the early vintage of the shot. Note the carved stone embellishments above the windows of the building.

46. Tramways staff pose at the entrance to the tram shed in 1903 with Manager Pilcher on the left, flanked by his deputy, Gilbert, and Alderman Robinson, Chairman of the Tramways Committee on the far right. Note the quasi-military uniforms then in vogue, in grey with red piping. The conductors lack only rifles to look the part of Ruritanian conscripts.

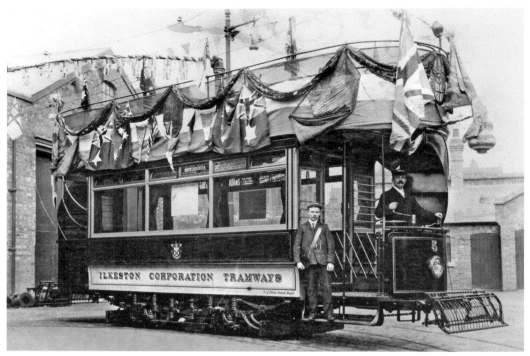

47. A superb study of Car 5 in the depot yard, decorated for the opening ceremony on May 16th 1903. The folded Stillgate lifeguard shows up well, as does the Corporation logo and coat of arms. Note the hanging paper lantern in front of the vehicle, whilst the diminutive conductor has yet to receive his uniform.

48. Car 5 stands at the entrance to the shed, which deployed four sets of tracks running into one, visible in the plan view of the site shown in plate 43. The photograph includes a fine view of the horse-drawn tower waggon, here shown in use with two linesmen at work on the overhead wiring.

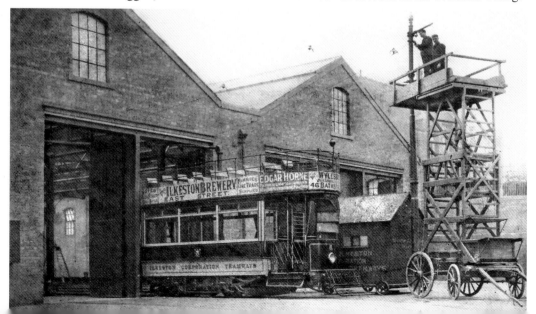

NOTTINGHAM ROAD

49. A post-tram view of the north-west end of Nottingham Road, with English Electric Trolleybus 302 (RB 5570) climbing the incline at its junction with Cavendish Road in May 1935. Note the feeder cables boosting power to the overhead, again carried on twin poles and span wire, for the uphill slope. Another trackless vehicle can be seen through the rear windows of the bus.

50. We look north up Nottingham Road around 1910, just below the junction with Dale Street, as bracket poles take over from the twin standards. Again the line runs centrally up the thoroughfare. The Catholic Presbytery can be seen in the centre distance, but not the church, which was not built until the 1920s.

51. The south-east end of Nottingham Road, again looking north in the 1920s, as a wealthy Il'sonian takes a spin in his splendid-looking Roller. The tram track can be seen between the two vehicles in the middle distance, swinging left into Thurman Street behind the strolling pedestrian. Brook Street leads off to the right.

THURMAN STREET

52. Just round the corner to the left from the previous view, English Electric Trolleybus 301 (RB 5569) turns off Nottingham Road onto Thurman Street and the Triangle on its way to Hallam Fields, with Brook Street visible behind.

CORPORATION ROAD

53. An evocative study of Car 4 coming off the Thurman Street loop on to Corporation Road. The curve by the Triangle can be seen in the left background, whilst the Wesleyan Chapel appears on the right. Some good detail stands out on this well-patronised conveyance, whose top-deck passengers are clearly posing for their pictures.

HALLAM FIELDS TERMINUS

54. At Hallam Fields terminus Cars 5 and 6 stand alongside each other on the inaugural run in May 1903, trolleybooms swung for the return journey in this relatively rural part of the system. The photograph shows well the clumsy cow catcher lifeguards, one folded, the other running along the track on small wheels.

55. The terminus provides a picturesque rustic scene as Car 9 awaits trade on the left-hand line outside St Bartholomew's Church. At both termini the track finished in an open ended stretch of twin rail to allow trams to stand side-by-side.

56. A rather dismal, wet day at Hallam Fields as Car 13 waits at the terminus outside the church. The long terrace of houses on the right was known as North View. Note the advertising shield on the tram standard, doubtless extolling the Mrs Bull magazine, companion to the popular John Bull.

57. Car 11 is caught in the countryside environment of Hallam Fields with the characteristics of the Milnes trams well displayed. Adverts are minimal, and the motorman seems well protected in oilskins and gauntlets, whilst the lower saloon still boasts curtains.

REFURBISHMENT

58.   In 1919-20 all the Ilkeston trams were renovated and repainted at the NDTC depot at Langley Mill. This shot of Car 3 shows the refurbishing staff, plus one of the inspectors and the altered staircases common to all cars returned to the Ilkeston branch.

59.   One of the overhauled tramcars is caught by the camera on Heanor Road, as the body is towed back into service, minus its truck and electrics, on a flat car behind William West's solid tyred haulier's lorry.

60. Gently decaying in the back garden of a Heanor Road residence is the lower saloon of one of the Ilkeston trams, sold off as a garden shed after the closure of the system. Many thousands of Il'sonians must have filled these utilitarian seats or stood strap hanging in this conveyance every week during its heyday, when it transported them along the streets of their native town.

PART 2 - GLOSSOP TRAMWAYS

Opening of the Electric Tramway	61	High Street West	88
Hadfield Terminus	66	Norfolk Square	94
Station Road	70	Victoria Street /	
Woolley Bridge Road	75	Charlestown Road Spur	103
Brookfield	77	High Street East	110
Dinting Vale	78	Hall Street	115
Dinting Tram Depot	83	Old Glossop Terminus	116

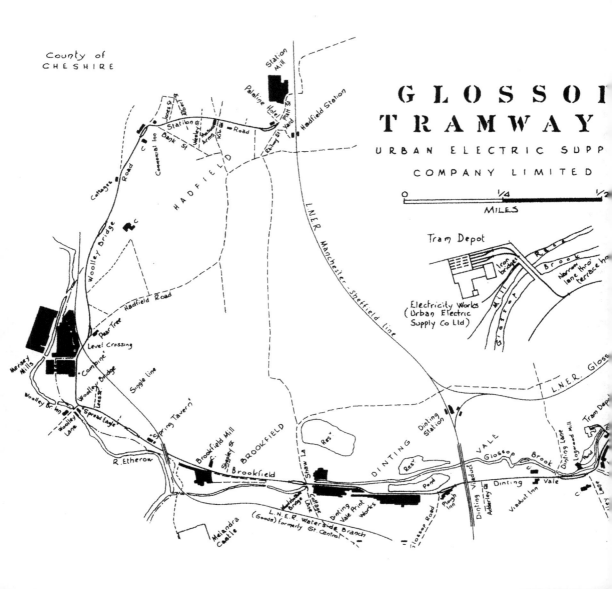

INTRODUCTION AND ACKNOWLEDGEMENTS

The Glossop Tramway opened on 21st August 1903, just over three months after that of Ilkeston, and was the second electric tramway in Derbyshire. It was a private enterprise run by the Urban Electricity Supply Company, who also owned the Camborne and Redruth Tramway in distant Cornwall.

For photographs of the Glossop Tramway I am deeply indebted to Sue Hickinson who has unstintingly provided me with a wealth of illustrations from her own extensive collection of Glossop pictures. I am also grateful to the Glossop Heritage Centre, Glossop Public Library, The Glossop and District Historical Society, Jim Bennett and A.K. Kirby for supplying other images of the system. Thanks are also due to Greg Fox for his plan of the undertaking, whilst Godfrey Croughton and Glynn Waite have kindly made available pictures of Glossop tickets from their collections.

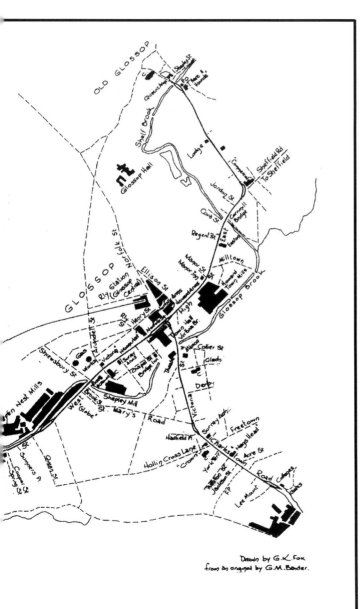

61. The Glossop line was in the form of an inverted 'C', with the main termini at Hadfield (top left) and Old Glossop (top right). The Whitfield spur terminated at the gates of Whitfield House (bottom right).

GEOGRAPHICAL SETTING

Situated in the extreme north-west of Derbyshire, in the gritstone hills of the South Pennines, Glossop is a long straggling community which is spread out along the Longdendale Valley. The strategic importance of the region was appreciated by the Romans, who built the auxiliary fort of *Ardotalia* (the fort on the brow), locally known as Melandra Castle, to command the route over the Pennines. The town consists of two separate elements, Hadfield and Glossop itself. Glossop was a mill town, and a number of cotton mills were scattered along the valley bottom, using water to supply the necessary motive power. It was felt that the tramway would provide quick access for employees to the various works and factories strung out along the route. The area was well served by the rail network, with the London and North Eastern Railway providing stations at Hadfield, Glossop and Dinting.

HISTORICAL BACKGROUND

Glossop was perhaps a surprising choice for an electric tramway, located as it was in a small and isolated mill town with a static population of some 22,000. It was presumably hoped that the enterprise would transport the large numbers of cotton workers who held jobs at the many factories along the route at a cheap rate. A further attraction was the possibility of a connection with the Stalybridge, Hyde, Mossley and Dukinfield Joint Board network (SHMD), whose lines, covering the eastern side of Manchester, ran as close as Mottram, a mere two miles (3.2 km) from Woolley Bridge on the county border.

The line was suggested by Glossop born Charles Knowles, who worked for the Urban Electricity Supply Company (UESC), and who was duly appointed engineer and manager of the project. In November 1900 the company applied for a provisional order to provide a tramway and an electricity supply to the town. The former was planned as an inverted 'C', four miles long, with the north-west terminus at Hadfield, and the north-east at Old Glossop, joining relatively undeveloped stretches of roadway studded with factories and large mills. A half-mile spur, known as the Whitfield branch, ran south of the main track to Charlestown.

The route was single track with turnouts, and was constructed to standard gauge, the same as the other tramway undertakings in the Manchester area. A site at Dinting on the north bank of the Glossop Brook was selected for the depot and power station, and by December 1902, tracklaying was under way. Seven open top, double deckers with reversed stairs were ordered from G.F. Milnes of Hadley, and were fitted with hard riding 6ft wheelbase German girder trucks. They were painted in dark green and primrose and bore the legend GLOSSOP TRAMWAYS on the rocker panels.

The power station was functional by August 1903 and the formal opening was set for the 20th. However the Board of Trade deferred this until the 21st, though the opening ceremony went ahead as scheduled. As with the Ilkeston enterprise, the early years were fruitful, though the Whitfield branch speedily proved a white elephant. In August 1904 Knowles purchased a one man, single deck demi-car, No.8, from the British Electric Car Company, which took over operations on the spur. The Glossop line never went into profit, and despite several attempts to secure a connection with the SHMD, the union never materialised; the most promising plan gained Royal Assent in 1915, but was killed off by the war.

In 1918 Knowles bought a further single-decker, an ex-Sheffield tram mounted on a 7ft (2133mm) Brill 21E truck. The vehicle had been extensively overhauled, and featured transverse seating. It went into service in March 1918, but it is not known whether it ever sported the Glossop livery, and no photographs of it operating in the town have so far surfaced.

By the early 1920s the facility was in urgent need of refurbishment and overhaul, and was also the subject of friction with the public, who felt that it was being run simply for commercial profit, with little regard for travellers. The Whitfield branch had closed in late 1918 as a wartime economy, and never reopened despite the council's demand that it should. The tram crews too were disgruntled as their working hours were cut, and their wages lagged behind the rising cost of living. The UESC tried to sell the undertaking to the council, who sensibly refused this millstone around their necks.

In June 1920 the car crews went on a ten day strike to improve their basic wages, but were forced back to work on the company's terms. By 1923 motorbuses were providing unwelcome competition along the tram route. Revenue fell steadily in the mid 1920s, and tramway mileage followed suit. In November 1927 the UESC offered the undertaking to the council as a gift, if the latter agreed to use the company power supply. When this was refused, the company announced the closure on Christmas Eve, 1927, a fine Christmas present to the tram crews! The last cars ran at 11pm that night, and on Boxing Day the North Western Road Car Company opened an omnibus service along the abandoned route. In April 1928 the UESC began lifting the tram track and reinstating the roadway, and a 24 year episode was finally closed.

OPENING OF THE ELECTRIC TRAMWAY

62. Motormen and conductors parade in smart 'maternity jacket' rig, including white-topped caps, in front of one of the new cars outside the Dinting tram shed at the start of the service. Superintendent Emmott takes the controls and on his right is Charles Knowles, the General Manager. A majority of the staff display fashionable hirsute adornment, whilst the Superintendent sports a full set!

63. In this shot the tramway staff show off a different rig, perhaps an alternative summer uniform. Two inspectors flank the nattily dressed but sadly unidentified gentleman in the centre of the photograph.

64. Although the tramway employees were male, World War I did necessitate the introduction of conductresses into service, including Mrs Alice Lee, seen here fully kitted out for duty in 1916.

65. Mr Squire Sellars, who owned a High Street East drapery and furnishing emporium, hired and decorated one of the cars for the opening day run on 21st August 1903. The tram can be seen outside his establishment, with senior staff posed on the top deck. Motorman James Phair stands alongside the platform, with an inspector at the controls. Mr Sellars is the central figure in the group to the right of the car, flanked by Superintendent Emmott and Salesman H. Crossley. The policeman on the far right is Constable White.

66. A superb side view of one of the brand-new tramcars from a postcard dated 11th September 1903, which picks out the salient features of the conveyance, including the livery, truck and track brake. Note the luxury of lower saloon curtaining.

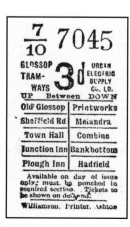

HADFIELD TERMINUS

67. The Hadfield terminus was situated on a loop immediately outside the Palatine and Railway Hotel opposite the LNER railway station. Here a service car and crew pose on the turnout, with Station Road on the left.

68. A good view of one of the trams at the terminus, with the trolleyboom as yet unswung for the return trip to town. The incline down Station Road can be clearly seen.

69. An evocative picture, with one of the Hadfield trams clearly unable to access the terminus loop due to the Empire Day celebrations on a sunny 24th May at the war memorial outside the library, dedicated on 26th March 1922. This dates the shot to between 1922-27. Among the considerable throng, controlled by a single policeman, a choir can be glimpsed below the lamppost at centre right.

FEB. 26, 1909.

GLOSSOP ELECTRIC TRAMWAYS.

IMPORTANT NOTICE.

With a view to improving the revenue, and to meet the wishes of the travelling public, I have pleasure in announcing that my directors have sanctioned the

RE-INTRODUCTION OF HALFPENNY FARES ON MARCH 1st.

This change is, however, to be considered in the nature of an experiment for a few months only, until it is seen whether the public take advantage of the reduced fares in sufficient numbers to warrant a permanent arrangement.

Workmen's Travelling Time in Morning will be Extended to 8-15 a.m.,

To meet the Convenience of School Teachers and Shop Assistants   Workmen's Reduced Fares during dinner hour (except on Saturdays) will be abolished.

WORKMEN'S RETURN TICKETS, available on day of issue only, will be introduced; the return half being available on any car during the day.

URBAN ELECTRIC SUPPLY COMPANY, Ltd.,
C. E. KNOWLES, Resident Engineer and Manager.

70. Taken just after the closure of the service, this view picks out a NWRCC double-decker bus outside the library on the left. The tramlines are still *in situ,* and the overhead is here carried on twin poles and span wire. Note the junction box at the base of the left hand post. This vista has changed surprisingly little over the years, apart from the inevitable intrusion of parked motor vehicles.

STATION ROAD

71. A short distance down Station Road Car 2, with a HADFIELD board hung on the dash, pauses on the hill on its way to the terminus. On the immediate left is Salisbury Street, with a hopeful passenger waiting beneath the stop sign on the bracket arm tram pole. The generally filthy state of the cobbled roadway is apparent in this view.

72. Just below the scene of the last picture Car 2, with HADFIELD this time painted round the dash lamp, poses for the camera outside Roberts' Music Stores. Note the offset trolleypole common to all the Milnes vehicles. In 2004 the shop on the extreme right was an Indian restaurant, a totally alien concept a hundred years ago when the shot was taken!

73. Car 3, well laden with young ladies perhaps on an outing, descends Station Road above Lambgates in the early years of the system. The board on the dash panel indicates that the tram serves both Old Glossop and the Whitfield spur. The fine twin-gabled building on the left still survives.

Form No. 90

THE URBAN ELECTRIC SUPPLY CO., LTD.

Head Office: BROAD SANCTUARY CHAMBERS, WESTMINSTER, S.W.

Engineers and Contractors:
EDMUNDSON'S ELECTRICITY
CORPORATION, LTD.

Resident Engineer:
C. E. KNOWLES.

Electricity Works, High Street West.
Office: 117, High Street West,
Glossop, August 10th 3. 190__

Messrs A. Williamson,
    Ticket Printers, etc.,
        Ashton U Lyne.

Dear Sirs,
    Referring to your quotations of July 22nd., kindly send us at once 10 Ticket Punches numbered consecutively.   We propose to take these on hire paying you a rental of 15/6 each per annum. Please despatch them per Passenger train tomorrow certain, so that I can practice the men in the use of them tomorrow evening.

        Yours faithfully,

URBAN ELECTRIC SUPPLY C
C. E. Knowles
RESIDENT ENG.

74. A last look along the upper part of Station Road, with Kiln Lane just visible on the right. The tram track takes the centre line of the cobbled street, and the running wire is carried here on bracket poles which were totally unadorned with wrought iron scrolling anywhere along the system.

75. A good view of the steep descent faced by passengers headed towards Glossop, with Wesley Street on the left, below the old Post Office. The photograph clearly shows the stone setts extending on both sides of the single line, and whose upkeep was the responsibility of the tramway company.

WOOLLEY BRIDGE ROAD

76.   Woolley Bridge Road took the tramline down into the valley bottom, and this view shows the track and overhead near the junction with John Dalton Street on the left. In the right hand distance can be seen the Pear Tree Inn.

77.   At the eastern end of Woolley Bridge Road the line, here offset to the side of the thoroughfare, took tramcars past John Walton's mill complex and a row of terraced cottages typical of many lining the route.

BROOKFIELD

78. The tramline ran alongside open fields at Brookfield, here shown with Brookfield Mill in the misty right-hand distance, and Shaw Lane on the right. Over the hill at the centre of the shot was Melandra Castle, the first century Roman fort, then under enthusiastic if generally uncritical excavation. The fort gave its name to one of the tram stops, perhaps a unique example. The early motorbus, N1081, evidently the subject of much interest, seems to have been on a trial run in 1905. Again the nearest tram standard carries a stop sign.

DINTING VALE

79. This view along Dinting Vale, looking towards Glossop, shows the tram track heading along the centreline of the road, and another set of typical stone terraces along the course of the system. Holy Trinity Church has disappeared in the mist.

80. Taken from the opposite direction, with Holy Trinity Church, a well loaded Car 7 heads for Hadfield. In the near distance is the spectacular Dinting Viaduct built in 1844, and seen in its original form before the addition of strengthening brick columns in 1918-19. Out of sight, round the corner on the extreme left is the Plough Inn, the halfway stage on the main route.

81. Tracklaying along the vale with Logwood Mill on the left and the Junction Inn on the distant right. The layout of the Junction loop can be seen at centre right. Note that the bracket poles have already been positioned, though the running wire has not yet been strung.

82. This view of the junction of Dinting Vale, which is seen on the left, with Simmondley Lane on the right and High Street West in the distance, shows the UESC tram shed and power station on the north bank of the Glossop Brook, with the Junction Inn on the extreme right of the shot.

83. A crowded Car 3, evidently on a short working from Woolley Bridge, prepares to enter High Street West with the tall chimney of the power station rising behind the tram. The location of this well known shot has often been misidentified, not least by myself!

DINTING TRAM DEPOT

84. The entrance to High Street West reveals the local Co-operative Shop on the right; between the distant terraces just above and to the right of the ambling dog, was the entrance to the tram depot.

85. The unimposing central gap between the terraces behind the cameraman's youthful audience, was the entrance to the tram shed, which was reached by a bridge over the Glossop Brook. Swann's fine clock on the left, now gone, shows the time at 12.16pm. Occupants of the houses on both sides of the entrance must have blessed the clanking which announced the start and end of daily services as the trams ground by at early and late hours!

86. The UESC had to build this iron bridge to span the brook to allow service cars to cross into High Street West. The depot and tram shed are on the left of this photograph.

87. This animated view shows the completed car shed in the distance, and reveals an early stage in the laying of the tramlines and feeder cables from the depot, which provided power and access for the undertaking.

88. A magnificent study of the depot complex dating from around 1910. To the left of the tall power station chimney can be seen the spire of Holy Trinity Church along Dinting Vale. The Glossop Brook iron bridge appears in the foreground, and on the right a tramcar stands in the depot yard.

HIGH STREET WEST

89. An excellent view shows Car 6 outside Latham's shop at 24 High Street West. Note the youthful conductor, and the concertina gate, which closed off the driver's platform. The oyster lamps, which provided illumination to the upper deck, stand at the head of each staircase.

90. Further along the widening town thoroughfare, looking east, Car 5 rattles towards Hadfield in the summer of 1905, with the now-gone Methodist Church nicknamed the 'Big Wesley' in shot on the right. Arundel Street is on the left, with the Victoria Inn sign visible on the street corner in a view that is still recognisable some hundred years later.

91. A close-up of the same car with a HADFIELD board on its dash panel, and a smart young-man-about-town on the left, with a double watch chain embellishing his waistcoat. Note the splendid hat on the lady behind him!

92. A little further east, a thinly populated street leads to the Town Hall, crowned with a clock tower, just behind George Street at the middle right. Apart from a single horse-and-cart, the thoroughfare is entirely clear of traffic.

93. Looking west, another view picks out a practically empty street, relieved only by the tramcar approaching the town centre along the gentle incline towards Norfolk Square. Note the sun blinds on the right - features that have now totally disappeared from modern shop frontages.

94. This original tramway junction box, in use until the 1980s, stood for some 80 years at the corner of Arundel and Surrey Streets, until its removal in April 1984.

NORFOLK SQUARE

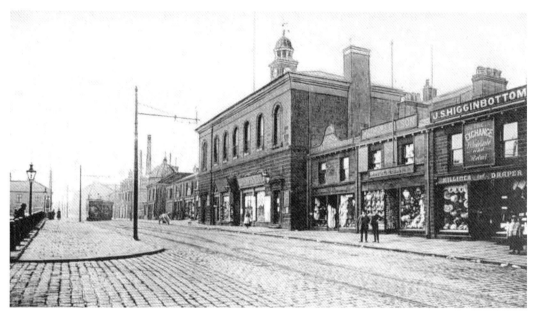

95. Norfolk Square was the hub of the tramway system, with cars departing for Hadfield, Old Glossop and, until 1918, Whitfield. In this scene, set amidst a sea of cobbles, two trams wait side-by-side on the lengthy turnout, with the Town Hall on the right.

96. A service car awaits customers for Hadfield in front of the Town Hall, with its turreted clock. The building was constructed in 1836-7 by the First Duke of Norfolk. Shops on the right include the Maypole Dairy, Buckley's Pawnbrokers and Hadfield's 'Athletic Outfitters'. The tall chimney and upperworks of Howard Town Mills loom up on the left.

97. Note Boot's Cash Chemists on the right, from whose premises this postcard was produced. A single car stands on the turnout, whose points show up well in the foreground, whilst the photographer has recruited a sample of the local youth to add variety to his composition.

98. A little further east in this post World War I view, the corner of Victoria Street can be seen just beyond the cupola, which bore several names during its lifetime. Above the glass verandah can be seen Jackson's Buildings, which date from 1900. The fleet number of the approaching tramcar has been obscured by the bracket pole, and on the extreme left is the sinister outline of a motorbus, a major threat to the viability of the ageing line.

99. The well filled double deck motorbus seen in photo 78 continues its merry way through Norfolk Square in 1905, passing a service car on the loop and Victoria Street on the left as it heads towards Old Glossop on an apparent proving run.

100. This 1923 picture was taken at the Norfolk Square crossroads, with Norfolk Street on the left, Victoria Street on the right and High Street East straight ahead. The branch tram tracks still swing right onto the Whitfield spur, and the overhead is still in place, though the line was abandoned in 1918 as a wartime economy. The notice in Hepworth's shop window announces closure during the Wakes Week holiday.

101. A decorated tramcar was pictured in Norfolk Square. The date and occasion are unknown, but the bells, portraits and garlands suggest it may celebrate a wedding, perhaps involving a member of the tramway staff. This theory is strengthened by the appearance of Superintendent Emmott, seen on the left. Note, however, that the Norfolk Hotel, seen in the left background, is also *en fete*.

102. No less than three tramcars can be spotted in this 1903 shot of the Square, including one on the left heading for Charlestown down Victoria Street. The heavily loaded woodcart is probably delivering logs from the station to Olive and Partington's paper mills. The cupola on the corner was at this time known as 'Bradbury's Corner' and housed a shaving saloon. A little earlier it was the location of Rosson's Chemists, and before its demolition in 1937 was nicknamed 'Hawley's Dome,' the premises of a local newsagents and stationers.

103. A final vista of the locality looking south down Norfolk Street reveals a vast swathe of cobblestones, plus carefully posed pedestrians and Car 1 heading down Victoria Street along the Whitworth spur line. The background to this postcard has been extensively retouched.

VICTORIA STREET/CHARLESTOWN ROAD SPUR

104. The BEC demi-car No.8, ordered for the branch line in 1904, is seen here on delivery, with Charles Knowles on the platform step. The lines of this boxy little 22 seater, with its prominent clerestory roof, show up well. Photographs suggest that the original truck - a set of railway waggon W-irons with a simple frame of bars to support the motors - was later replaced with a more sophisticated model.

105. An interesting close-up looking north down Victoria Street shows a pre-World War I Church Walk, and picks out the little demi-car caught among the worshippers. Immediately behind it an open-top tram moves west along High Street with two ladies occupying the upper deck front seats. The nearest tram standard carries a variant style of stop sign.

106. Looking in the other direction from the last illustration, the camera discloses the rustic theatre on the right, with a tramcar descending Victoria Street behind the horse and trap, on its way to Norfolk Square from Charlestown. On 24th March 1904, an out-of-control tram careered down this slope, hurtled across High Street and hit the pavement outside Shoebridge's shop, though thankfully no one was seriously hurt in the incident.

107. A service car grinds laboriously up Victoria Street on the way to Charlestown, with the tower of Littlemoor Sunday School on the right, behind a row of typical Glossop stone terraces. The gentleman at lower left, thumbs hooked in his waistcoat, seems determined to get in the picture.

108. Taken at the highest point of the road just above Derby Street, this scene looks towards town down the slope. Note the usual type of stop sign on the nearest bracket pole, and the milk cart in the middle distance. Again, the Shire horse on the right was probably from the stable of Olive and Partington's paper mill.

109. This superb study is of Demi-Car 8 at the Charlestown Road terminus loop at what is now the entrance to Glossop Fire Station. Standing alongside is Motorman John Byrom in appropriate heavy duty footwear. The photograph captures the main features of this little pay-as-you-enter tramcar to perfection, and a comparison with picture 104 shows a different type of truck to the former.

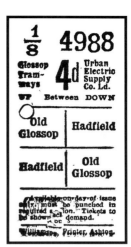

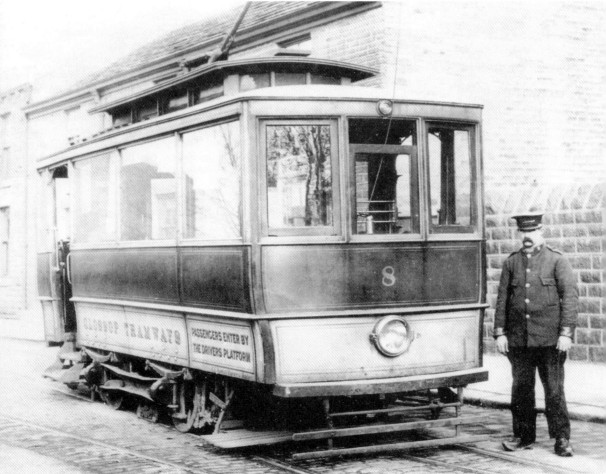

HIGH STREET EAST

110. A view west along the western end of this street shows the Town Hall clock tower, with a glimpse of Bradbury's Dome peeping out below it. Beneath the flagpole on the right is Squire Sellars' emporium, and the Howard Arms is just out of sight on the extreme right. Just to the left of Sellar's shop is the Glossop Co-operative building.

111. Taken from the opposite direction, this illustration shows well the arrangement of stone setts in which the tramlines were laid. On the right is the long-gone Yorkshire Terrace, and on the left London House advertises petrol and Rover and Napier motor cars. In the distance the roadway swings left beyond the three horse carts.

112. The eastern end of High Street East again gives way to rows of stone terraced houses along the line of the tramway. In the distance the Commercial Hotel can just be glimpsed as the tram tracks curve hard left on to Hall Street and the final stretch of the main line. Note the four proud mothers displaying bouncing babies for the photographer.

113. The cameraman set up his gear at the corner of High Street East (behind the tram), and Hall Street on the right. In this picture the car is Glossop bound, whilst the local children scatter themselves around the ornamental wrought iron fountain.

114. In this photograph, taken at the same time as the last, the locals cluster on and around the fountain as another tram, bearing OLD GLOSSOP AND HADFIELD on its dash, pauses on its way to the former destination. The line of High Street East heads into the distance on the left.

HALL STREET

115. The junction of High Street East and Hall Street (renamed Manor Park Road in 1926) had a loop laid on the bend, which Car 6 is just entering on its way from Old Glossop. The Commercial Hotel is on the right, and the fine drinking fountain supporting a streetlamp, and now long gone, was erected through the generosity of Mrs John Wood who lived at Whitfield House. Note the feeder box alongside the left hand bracket pole.

OLD GLOSSOP TERMINUS

116. The Old Glossop terminus, showing two of the three public houses sited nearby, the Talbot Inn, with the Hare and Hounds behind. The line terminated in a loop, as at Hadfield and Charlestown, with a short length of single line in front of the horse's hoofs.

117. On opening day a laden Car 3 prepares to leave Old Glossop on its inaugural run. The third of the trio of nearby public houses, The Queen's Arms, is on the right, and the landlord doubtless contemplates increased profits from disembarking riders as he poses in the doorway of his tavern. The little boy on the top deck is C.C. Walker, shown together with his parents, and his sister on his left. The tram conductor rejoiced in the nickname of 'Masher' Howard, though whether this related to his pugilistic or sartorial accomplishments is unknown.

118. The inevitable Car 3 is seen in close-up at Old Glossop with the Queen's Arms behind, showing the HADFIELD destination painted round the dashlamp, and other interesting details of the tram and its crew.

Form No. 81

THE URBAN ELECTRIC SUPPLY COMPANY, LIMITED.
HEAD OFFICE: BROAD SANCTUARY CHAMBERS, WESTMINSTER, S.W.

ENGINEERS AND CONTRACTORS
EDMUNDSONS ELECTRICITY
CORPORATION LTD

RESIDENT ENGINEER
C. E. KNOWLES.

BRANCHES
CAMBORNE
REDRUTH
GLOSSOP
TWICKENHAM
HAWICK
GRANTHAM
BERWICK ON TWEED
CATERHAM
GODALMING
NEWTON ABBOT
STAMFORD
DARTMOUTH
WEYBRIDGE
NEWBURY

Electricity Works, High Street West.
Office: 117, High Street West,
Glossop, Sept. 15th 1903.   190

Mr A. Williamson,
   Ticket printer,
     Ashton U. Lyne.

Dear Sir,   Re. Two Sample Bell Punches.

In reply to your favour of the 14th inst., I still have these on hand, as you rightly suppose. A few days' ago I found it necessary to put on an extra Conductor, and have allowed him to use the punch you kindly sent to us on loan until I was satisfied that we should require one permanently.

I find that it will be necessary to keep 11 punches in constant use, and I shall be glad if you will kindly send me another punch numbered 1924 so that it may follow in the same sequence as the 10 you sent us on August 11th. We shall require these on the hire system like the others. On receipt of this new punch, I will return the one on loan together with the mechanism belonging the other one which you kindly sent for our examination.

          Yours faithfully,
          C. E. Knowles

119. In 1918 the tramway took delivery of an ex-Sheffield single decker, No.56, seen here in earlier service in the city. The 'SV' sign indicated its usual city route as Spring Vale. The tram featured transverse seating and drop windows. No views exist of this car in Glossop service, and details of its numbering and livery are unknown.

120. After the closure of the tramway, the car bodies were sold off locally. One of them, apparently Demi-Car 8 by the look of the roof, saw service as part of a hairdressing salon in a building alongside the Spread Eagle Inn at Woolley Bridge. This shot was taken in the 1970s, before the structure was demolished.

Middleton Press — Easebourne Lane, Midhurst, West Sussex. GU29 9AZ

A-0 906520   B-1 873793   C-1 901706   D-1 904474

OOP Out of Print - Please check current availability   **BROCHURE AVAILABLE SHOWING NEW TITLES**
Tel: 01730 813169   www.middletonpress.com   sales@middletonpress.co.uk

A
- Abergavenny to Merthyr C 91 5
- Aldgate & Stepney Tramways B 70 7
- Allhallows - Branch Line to A 62 2
- Alton - Branch Lines to A 11 8
- Andover to Southampton A 82 7
- Ascot - Branch Lines around A 64 9
- Ashburton - Branch Line to B 95 2
- Ashford - Steam to Eurostar B 67 7
- Ashford to Dover A 48 7
- Austrian Narrow Gauge D 04 7
- Avonmouth - BL around D 42 X

B
- Banbury to Birmingham D 27 6
- Barking to Southend C 80 X
- Barnet & Finchley Tramways B 93 6
- Basingstoke to Salisbury A 89 4
- Bath Green Park to Bristol C 36 2
- Bath to Evercreech Junction A 60 6
- Bath Tramways B 86 3
- Battle over Portsmouth 1940 A 29 0
- Battle over Sussex 1940 A 79 7
- Bedford to Wellingborough D 31 4
- Betwixt Petersfield & Midhurst A 94 0
- Blitz over Sussex 1941-42 B 35 9
- Bodmin - Branch Lines around B 83 9
- Bognor at War 1939-45 B 59 6
- Bombers over Sussex 1943-45 B 51 0
- Bournemouth & Poole Trys B 47 2 OOP
- Bournemouth to Evercreech Jn A 46 0
- Bournemouth to Weymouth A 57 6
- Bournemouth Trolleybuses C 10 9
- Bradford Trolleybuses D 19 5
- Brecon to Neath D 43 8
- Brecon to Newport D 16 0
- Brickmaking in Sussex B 19 7
- Brightons Tramways B 02 2
- Brighton to Eastbourne A 16 9
- Brighton to Worthing A 03 7
- Bristols Tramways B 57 X
- Bristol to Taunton D 03 9
- Bromley South to Rochester B 23 5 OOP
- Bude - Branch Line to B 29 4
- Burnham to Evercreech Jn A 68 1
- Burton & Ashby Tramways C 51 6

C
- Camberwell & West Norwood TW B 22 7
- Canterbury - Branch Lines around B 58 8
- Caterham & Tattenham Corner B 25 1
- Changing Midhurst C 15 X
- Chard and Yeovil - BLs around C 30 3
- Charing Cross to Dartford A 75 4
- Charing Cross to Orpington A 96 7
- Cheddar - Branch Line to B 90 1
- Cheltenham to Andover C 43 5
- Chesterfield Tramways D 37 3
- Chichester to Portsmouth A 14 2 OOP
- Clapham & Streatham Tramways B 97 9
- Clapham Junction - 50 yrs C 06 0
- Clapham Junction to Beckenham Jn B 36 7
- Clevedon & Portishead - BLs to D 18 7
- Collectors Trains, Trolleys & Trams D 29 2
- Crawley to Littlehampton A 34 7
- Cromer - Branch Lines around C 26 5
- Croydons Tramways B 42 5
- Croydons Trolleybuses B 73 1
- Croydon to East Grinstead B 48 0
- Crystal Palace (HL) & Catford Loop A 87 8

D
- Darlington Trolleybuses D 33 0
- Dartford to Sittingbourne B 34 0
- Derby Tramways D 17 9
- Derby Trolleybuses C 72 9
- Derwent Valley - Branch Line to the D 06 3
- Didcot to Banbury D 02 0
- Didcot to Swindon C 84 2
- Didcot to Winchester C 13 3
- Douglas to Peel C 88 5
- Douglas to Port Erin C 55 9
- Douglas to Ramsey D 39 X
- Dover's Tramways B 24 3
- Dover to Ramsgate A 78 9

E
- Ealing to Slough C 42 7
- Eastbourne to Hastings A 27 4 OOP
- East Croydon to Three Bridges A 53 3
- East Grinstead - Branch Lines to A 07 X
- East Ham & West Ham Tramways B 52 9
- East Kent Light Railway A 61 4
- East London - Branch Lines of C 44 3
- East London Line B 80 4
- East Ridings Secret Resistance D 21 7
- Edgware & Willesden Tramways C 18 4
- Effingham Junction - BLs around A 74 6
- Eltham & Woolwich Tramways B 74 X
- Ely to Kings Lynn C 53 2
- Ely to Norwich C 90 7
- Embankment & Waterloo Tramways B 41 3
- Enfield & Wood Green Trys C 03 6 OOP
- Enfield Town & Palace Gates - BL to D 32 2
- Epsom to Horsham A 30 4
- Euston to Harrow & Wealdstone C 89 3
- Exeter & Taunton Tramways B 32 4
- Exeter to Barnstaple B 15 4
- Exeter to Newton Abbot C 49 4
- Exeter to Tavistock B 69 3
- Exmouth - Branch Lines to B 00 6 OOP

F
- Fairford - Branch Line to A 52 5
- Falmouth, Helston & St. Ives - BL to C 74 5
- Fareham to Salisbury A 67 3
- Faversham to Dover B 05 7 OOP
- Felixstowe & Aldeburgh - BL to D 20 9
- Fenchurch Street to Barking C 20 6
- Festiniog - 50 yrs of change C 83 4
- Festiniog in the Fifties B 68 5
- Festiniog in the Sixties B 91 X
- Finsbury Park to Alexandra Palace C 02 8
- Frome to Bristol B 77 4
- Fulwell - Trams, Trolleys & Buses D 11 X

G
- Garraway Father & Son A 20 7 OOP
- Gloucester to Bristol D 35 7
- Gosport & Horndean Trys B 92 8 OOP
- Gosport - Branch Lines around A 36 3
- Great Yarmouth Tramways D 13 6
- Greenwich & Dartford Tramways B 14 6
- Guildford to Redhill A 63 0

H
- Hammersmith & Hounslow Trys C 33 8
- Hampshire Narrow Gauge D 36 5
- Hampshire Waterways A 84 3 OOP
- Hampstead & Highgate Tramways B 53 7
- Harrow to Watford D 14 4
- Hastings to Ashford A 37 1 OOP
- Hastings Tramways B 18 9
- Hastings Trolleybuses B 81 2
- Hawkhurst - Branch Line to A 66 5
- Hayling - Branch Line to A 12 6
- Haywards Heath to Seaford A 28 2 OOP
- Henley, Windsor & Marlow - BL to C77 X
- Hitchin to Peterborough D 07 1
- Holborn & Finsbury Tramways B 79 0
- Holborn Viaduct to Lewisham A 81 9
- Horsham - Branch Lines to A 02 9
- Huddersfield Trolleybuses C 92 3
- Hull Trolleybuses D 24 1
- Huntingdon - Branch Lines around A 93 2

I
- Ilford & Barking Tramways B 61 8
- Ilford to Shenfield C 97 4
- Ilfracombe - Branch Line to B 21 9
- Ilkeston & Glossop Tramways D 40 3
- Industrial Rlys of the South East A 09 6
- Ipswich to Saxmundham C 41 9
- Isle of Wight Lines - 50 yrs C 12 5

K
- Kent & East Sussex Waterways A 72 X
- Kent Narrow Gauge C 45 1
- Kingsbridge - Branch Line to C 98 2
- Kingston & Hounslow Loops A 83 5
- Kingston & Wimbledon Tramways B 56 1
- Kingswear - Branch Line to C 17 6

L
- Lambourn - Branch Line to C 70 2
- Launceston & Princetown - BL to C 19 2
- Lewisham & Catford Tramways B 26 X
- Lewisham to Dartford A 92 4 OOP

- Lines around Wimbledon B 75 8
- Liverpool Street to Chingford D 01 2
- Liverpool Street to Ilford C 34 6
- Liverpool Tramways - Eastern C 04 4
- Liverpool Tramways - Northern C 46 X
- Liverpool Tramways - Southern C 23 0
- London Bridge to Addiscombe B 20 0
- London Bridge to East Croydon A 58 4
- London Chatham & Dover Rly A 88 6
- London Termini - Past and Proposed D 00 4
- London to Portsmouth Waterways B 43 X
- Longmoor - Branch Lines to A 41 X
- Looe - Branch Line to C 22 2
- Lyme Regis - Branch Line to A 45 2
- Lynton - Branch Line to B 04 9

M
- Maidstone & Chatham Tramways B 40 5
- Maidstone Trolleybuses C 00 1 OOP
- March - Branch Lines around B 09 X
- Margate & Ramsgate Tramways C 52 4
- Midhurst - Branch Lines around A 49 5
- Midhurst - Branch Lines to A 01 0 OOP
- Military Defence of West Sussex A 23 1
- Military Signals, South Coast C 54 0
- Minehead - Branch Line to A 80 0
- Mitcham Junction Lines B 01 4
- Mitchell & company C 59 1 OOP
- Moreton-in-Marsh to Worcester D 26 8
- Moretonhampstead - Branch Line to C 27 3

N
- Newbury to Westbury C 66 4
- Newport - Branch Lines to A 26 6
- Newquay - Branch Lines to C 71 0
- Newton Abbot to Plymouth C 60 5
- Northern France Narrow Gauge C 75 3
- North Kent Tramways B 44 8
- North London Line B 94 4
- North Woolwich - BLs around C 65 6
- Norwich Tramways C 40 0

O
- Orpington to Tonbridge B 03 0
- Oxford to Moreton-in-Marsh D 15 2

P
- Paddington to Ealing C 37 0
- Paddington to Princes Risborough C 81 8
- Padstow - Branch Line to B 54 5
- Plymouth - BLs around B 98 7
- Plymouth to St. Austell C 63 X
- Porthmadog 1954-94 - BL around B 31 6
- Porthmadog to Blaenau B 50 2 OOP
- Portmadoc 1923-46 - BL around B 13 8
- Portsmouths Tramways B 72 3 OOP
- Portsmouth to Southampton A 31 2
- Portsmouth Trolleybuses C 73 7
- Princes Risborough - Branch Lines to D 05 5
- Princes Risborough to Banbury C 85 0

R
- Railways to Victory C 16 8
- Reading to Basingstoke B 27 8
- Reading to Didcot C 79 6
- Reading to Guildford A 47 9
- Reading Tramways B 87 1
- Reading Trolleybuses C 05 2
- Redhill to Ashford A 73 8
- Return to Blaenau 1970-82 C 64 8
- Roman Roads of Surrey C 61 3
- Roman Roads of Sussex C 48 6
- Romneyrail C 32 X
- Ryde to Ventnor A 19 3

S
- Salisbury to Westbury B 39 1
- Salisbury to Yeovil B 06 5
- Saxmundham to Yarmouth C 69 9
- Seaton & Eastbourne T/Ws B 76 6 OOP
- Seaton & Sidmouth - Branch Lines to A 95 9
- Secret Sussex Resistance B 82 0
- SECR Centenary album C 11 7
- Selsey - Branch Line to A 04 5 OOP
- Sheerness - Branch Lines around B 16 2
- Shepherds Bush to Uxbridge T/Ws C 28 1
- Shrewsbury - Branch Line to A 86 X
- Sierra Leone Narrow Gauge D 28 4
- Sittingbourne to Ramsgate A 90 8
- Slough to Newbury C 56 7

- Southamptons Tramways B 33 2 OOP
- Southampton to Bournemouth A 42 8
- Southend-on-Sea Tramways B 28 6
- Southern France Narrow Gauge C 47 8
- Southwark & Deptford Tramways B 38
- Southwold - Branch Line to A 15 0
- South Eastern & Chatham Railways C
- South London Line B 46 4
- South London Tramways 1903-33 D 10
- St. Albans to Bedford D 08 X
- St. Austell to Penzance C 67 2
- St. Pancras to St. Albans C 78 8
- Stamford Hill Tramways B 85 5
- Steaming through Cornwall B 30 8
- Steaming through Kent A 13 4
- Steaming through the Isle of Wight A 56
- Steaming through West Hants A 69 X
- Stratford-upon-Avon to Cheltenham C
- Strood to Paddock Wood B 12 X
- Surrey Home Guard C 57 5
- Surrey Narrow Gauge C 87 X
- Surrey Waterways A 51 7 OOP
- Sussex Home Guard C 24 9
- Sussex Narrow Gauge C 68 0
- Sussex Shipping Sail, Steam & Motor D
- Swanley to Ashford B 45 6
- Swindon to Bristol C 96 5
- Swindon to Newport D 30 6
- Swiss Narrow Gauge C 94 X

T
- Talyllyn - 50 years C 39 7
- Taunton to Barnstaple B 60 X 3
- Taunton to Exeter C 82 6
- Tavistock to Plymouth B 88 X
- Tenterden - Branch Line to A 21 5
- Thanet's Tramways B 11 1 OOP
- Three Bridges to Brighton A 35 5
- Tilbury Loop C 86 9
- Tiverton - Branch Lines around C 62 1
- Tivetshall to Beccles D 41 1
- Tonbridge to Hastings A 44 4
- Torrington - Branch Lines to B 37 5
- Tunbridge Wells - Branch Lines to C 32
- Twickenham & Kingston Trys C 35 4
- Two-Foot Gauge Survivors C 21 4 OOP

U
- Upwell - Branch Line to B 64 2

V
- Victoria & Lambeth Tramways B 49 9
- Victoria to Bromley South A 98 3
- Victoria to East Croydon A 40 1
- Vivarais C 31 1

W
- Walthamstow & Leyton Tramways B 65
- Waltham Cross & Edmonton Trys C 07
- Wandsworth & Battersea Tramways B
- Wantage - Branch Line to D 25 X
- Wareham to Swanage - 50 yrs D 09 8
- War on the Line A 10 X
- Waterloo to Windsor A 54 1
- Waterloo to Woking A 38 X
- Wenford Bridge to Fowey C 09 5
- Westbury to Bath B 55 3
- Westbury to Taunton C 76 1
- West Croydon to Epsom B 08 1
- West London - Branch Lines of C 50 8
- West London Line B 84 7
- West Sussex Waterways A 24 X
- West Wiltshire - Branch Lines of D 12 8
- Weymouth - Branch Lines around A 65
- Willesden Junction to Richmond B 71 5
- Wimbledon to Beckenham C 58 3
- Wimbledon to Epsom B 62 6
- Wimborne - Branch Lines around A 97 5
- Wisbech - Branch Lines around C 01 X
- Wisbech 1800-1901 C 93 1
- Woking to Alton A 59 2
- Woking to Portsmouth A 25 8
- Woking to Southampton A 55 X
- Woolwich & Dartford Trolleys B 66 9 OOP
- Worcester to Hereford D 38 1
- Worthing to Chichester A 06 1 OOP

Y
- Yeovil - 50 yrs change C 38 9
- Yeovil to Dorchester A 76 2
- Yeovil to Exeter A 91 6